# MACHINE LEARNING

Complete Crash Course with Test Q&A

Yatendra Kumar Singh 'Manuh'

# CONTENTS

# INTRODUCTION

Welcome to **"Machine Learning - Complete Crash Course with Test Q&A"**, your comprehensive guide to mastering the fascinating world of machine learning. This book is designed to equip you with the essential knowledge and skills needed to understand, build, and evaluate machine learning models, preparing you for certification and real-world applications.

**Why Machine Learning?**

Machine learning is revolutionizing various industries, from healthcare and finance to marketing and transportation. It empowers computers to learn from data and make intelligent decisions, leading to innovations that enhance our daily lives. Whether you're a budding data scientist, a software engineer looking to expand your skill set, or a professional seeking to leverage machine learning in your field, this course is your gateway to unlocking the potential of this transformative technology.

**What You Will Learn**

This crash course is structured into 11 comprehensive chapters, each focusing on a crucial aspect of machine learning. Here's a glimpse of what you'll explore:

1. **Introduction to Machine Learning**: Understand the fundamentals, history, and types of machine learning.

2. **Data Preprocessing and Exploration**: Learn how to prepare and explore your data for meaningful insights.

3. **Supervised Learning - Regression**: Dive into linear, polynomial, and regularized regression techniques.

4. **Supervised Learning - Classification**: Master classification algorithms like logistic regression, SVM, and decision trees.

5. **Unsupervised Learning**: Explore clustering, dimensionality reduction, and anomaly detection.

6. **Neural Networks and Deep Learning**: Discover the power of neural networks, CNNs, RNNs, and deep learning frameworks.

7. **Reinforcement Learning**: Delve into the fundamentals and applications of reinforcement learning.

8. **Model Selection and Optimization**: Learn cross-validation, hyperparameter tuning, and model ensembling techniques.

9. **Model Deployment and Maintenance**: Understand strategies for deploying, monitoring, and maintaining models in production.

10. **Ethical and Responsible AI**: Explore fairness, bias, privacy, and interpretability in AI.

11. **Capstone Project**: Apply your knowledge to a real-world problem, from project selection to deployment.

**Interactive Learning with Test Q&A**

Each chapter concludes with a set of test questions and answers, allowing you to assess your understanding and reinforce your learning. These questions are designed to challenge your knowledge and help you prepare for certification exams.

## Getting Started

No prior experience in machine learning? No problem! This course starts with the basics and gradually builds up to advanced topics. Whether you're a beginner or have some experience, you'll find this course valuable and engaging.

Embark on this learning journey and discover the exciting possibilities that machine learning offers. Let's dive in and start transforming data into intelligence!

# CHAPTER 1: INTRODUCTION TO MACHINE LEARNING

## 1.1 What is Machine Learning?

- **Definition**: Machine Learning (ML) is a subfield of artificial intelligence (AI) that focuses on developing algorithms and statistical models that enable computers to perform specific tasks without explicit instructions.

- **Concepts**:
  - Learning from data
  - Making predictions or decisions
  - Improving performance over time

# 1.2 HISTORY AND EVOLUTION

- **Early Beginnings**:
  - ○ 1950s: Arthur Samuel's work on checkers
  - ○ 1957: Perceptron model by Frank Rosenblatt
- **Key Milestones**:
  - ○ 1980s: Development of neural networks
  - ○ 1990s: Introduction of support vector machines (SVM)
  - ○ 2000s: Rise of big data and deep learning
- **Modern Era**:
  - ○ 2010s: Breakthroughs in deep learning and AI applications

# 1.3 TYPES OF MACHINE LEARNING

- **Supervised Learning**:
  - Learning from labeled data
  - Examples: Classification, Regression
- **Unsupervised Learning**:
  - Finding patterns in unlabeled data
  - Examples: Clustering, Dimensionality Reduction
- **Reinforcement Learning**:
  - Learning through trial and error
  - Examples: Game playing, Robotics

# 1.4 APPLICATIONS OF MACHINE LEARNING IN VARIOUS FIELDS

- **Healthcare**: Disease diagnosis, Personalized treatment
- **Finance**: Fraud detection, Algorithmic trading
- **Marketing**: Customer segmentation, Recommendation systems
- **Transportation**: Autonomous vehicles, Traffic prediction
- **Others**: Natural Language Processing (NLP), Image and Speech Recognition

# 1.5 COURSE OVERVIEW AND CERTIFICATION REQUIREMENTS

- **Course Objectives**:
    - Understand fundamental ML concepts
    - Gain practical experience with ML algorithms
    - Develop skills to implement ML solutions
- **Certification Requirements**:
    - Complete all course modules
    - Submit and pass capstone project
    - Score above 70% on final exam

# TEST QUESTIONS
# AND ANSWERS

# MULTIPLE CHOICE QUESTIONS

1. **What is the primary goal of machine learning?**
    - ◦ A. To understand human language
    - ◦ B. To make computers perform tasks without explicit instructions
    - ◦ C. To build faster computers
    - ◦ D. To create new hardware devices

**Answer:** B

2. **Which of the following is an example of supervised learning?**
    - ◦ A. K-Means Clustering
    - ◦ B. Principal Component Analysis (PCA)
    - ◦ C. Linear Regression
    - ◦ D. Autoencoders

**Answer:** C

3. **What is reinforcement learning primarily used for?**
    - ◦ A. Image Classification
    - ◦ B. Text Generation
    - ◦ C. Learning through trial and error
    - ◦ D. Reducing data dimensionality

**Answer:** C

# TRUE OR FALSE

1. **Machine learning models improve their performance over time by learning from data.**

**Answer**: True

2. **Unsupervised learning requires labeled data for training the models.**

**Answer**: False

3. **The perceptron model was introduced in the 1950s.**

**Answer**: True

# SHORT ANSWER QUESTIONS

1. **Explain the difference between supervised and unsupervised learning.**

   - **Answer**: Supervised learning involves training a model on labeled data, where the output is known, and the goal is to predict the output for new data. Unsupervised learning involves finding patterns in unlabeled data without predefined outputs.

2. **Name two key milestones in the history of machine learning.**

   - **Answer**:
       1. Introduction of the perceptron model by Frank Rosenblatt in 1957.
       2. Rise of deep learning and AI applications in the 2010s.

3. **List two applications of machine learning in healthcare.**

   - **Answer**:
       1. Disease diagnosis
       2. Personalized treatment

# CHAPTER 2: DATA PREPROCESSING AND EXPLORATION

## 2.1 Understanding Data Types and Structures

- **Data Types**:
  - **Numerical**: Continuous (e.g., age, salary) and Discrete (e.g., number of children)
  - **Categorical**: Nominal (e.g., color, gender) and Ordinal (e.g., rankings)
- **Data Structures**:
  - **Tabular Data**: Tables with rows and columns (e.g., spreadsheets, CSV files)
  - **Time Series Data**: Data points indexed by time (e.g., stock prices, weather data)
  - **Text Data**: Unstructured data in the form of text (e.g., articles, tweets)
  - **Image Data**: Pixel values representing images (e.g., photos, medical scans)

# 2.2 DATA CLEANING TECHNIQUES

- **Handling Missing Values**:
    - Imputation (mean, median, mode)
    - Deleting rows or columns
- **Handling Outliers**:
    - Identification using statistical methods (e.g., Z-score, IQR)
    - Removal or transformation of outliers
- **Dealing with Duplicates**:
    - Identifying and removing duplicate records
- **Data Transformation**:
    - Normalization and standardization
    - Encoding categorical variables (e.g., one-hot encoding, label encoding)

# 2.3 FEATURE ENGINEERING AND SELECTION

- **Feature Engineering**:
    - Creating new features from existing ones
    - Feature extraction techniques
- **Feature Selection**:
    - Filter methods (e.g., correlation coefficient)
    - Wrapper methods (e.g., recursive feature elimination)
    - Embedded methods (e.g., Lasso regression)

# 2.4 EXPLORATORY DATA ANALYSIS (EDA)

- **Descriptive Statistics**:
  - Measures of central tendency (mean, median, mode)
  - Measures of dispersion (range, variance, standard deviation)
- **Data Visualization**:
  - Histograms and bar plots
  - Box plots and scatter plots
  - Heatmaps and pair plots
- **Identifying Patterns and Relationships**:
  - Correlation analysis
  - Finding trends and anomalies

# 2.5 DATA VISUALIZATION TOOLS AND TECHNIQUES

- **Tools**:
    - Matplotlib
    - Seaborn
    - Plotly
    - Tableau
- **Techniques**:
    - Choosing the right chart type for the data
    - Using color, size, and shape to enhance readability
    - Creating interactive visualizations

# TEST QUESTIONS
# AND ANSWERS

# MULTIPLE CHOICE QUESTIONS

1. **Which of the following is an example of numerical data?**
    - ◦ A. Gender
    - ◦ B. Age
    - ◦ C. Color
    - ◦ D. Rankings

**Answer:** B

2. **What is the purpose of data normalization?**
    - ◦ A. To remove duplicates
    - ◦ B. To handle missing values
    - ◦ C. To scale numerical features to a common range
    - ◦ D. To encode categorical variables

**Answer:** C

3. **Which method can be used to identify outliers in a dataset?**
    - ◦ A. One-hot encoding
    - ◦ B. Z-score
    - ◦ C. Mean imputation
    - ◦ D. Correlation coefficient

**Answer:** B

# TRUE OR FALSE

1. **Tabular data is represented in the form of rows and columns.**

**Answer**: True

2. **Label encoding is a technique used to handle missing values.**

**Answer**: False

3. **Exploratory Data Analysis (EDA) involves using statistical methods and visualization techniques to understand data.**

**Answer**: True

# SHORT ANSWER QUESTIONS

1. **What is the difference between normalization and standardization?**
   - **Answer**: Normalization scales the data to a fixed range, typically [0, 1], while standardization scales the data to have a mean of 0 and a standard deviation of 1.

2. **Name two data visualization tools commonly used in machine learning.**
   - **Answer**:
     1. Matplotlib
     2. Seaborn

3. **Explain the purpose of feature selection in machine learning.**
   - **Answer**: Feature selection aims to identify the most relevant features for a machine learning model to improve its performance, reduce overfitting, and enhance interpretability.

# CHAPTER 3: SUPERVISED LEARNING – REGRESSION

## 3.1 Linear Regression

- **Definition**: Linear regression is a simple and widely used technique for predicting a continuous target variable based on one or more predictor variables by fitting a linear relationship.

- **Mathematical Representation**:
  - Simple Linear Regression: $y = \beta_0 + \beta_1 x + \epsilon$
  - Multiple Linear Regression: $y = \beta_0 + \beta_1 x_1 + \beta_2 x_2 + \dots + \beta_n x_n + \epsilon$
  - Where $y$ is the target variable, $x$ is the predictor variable(s), $\beta_0$ is the intercept, $\beta_1, \beta_2, \dots, \beta_n$ are the coefficients, and $\epsilon$ is the error term.

- **Assumptions**:
  - Linearity: The relationship between the predictors and the target variable is linear.
  - Independence: Observations are independent of

each other.

- Homoscedasticity: The variance of the residuals is constant.
- Normality: The residuals are normally distributed.

- **Evaluation Metrics**:
  - Mean Absolute Error (MAE)
  - Mean Squared Error (MSE)
  - Root Mean Squared Error (RMSE)
  - R-squared (R2R^2)

# 3.2 POLYNOMIAL REGRESSION

- **Definition**: Polynomial regression is a form of regression that models the relationship between the target variable and the predictor variables as an nth degree polynomial.

- **Mathematical Representation**:
  - $y = \beta_0 + \beta_1 x + \beta_2 x^2 + \ldots + \beta_n x^n + \epsilon$

- **Applications**:
  - When the relationship between variables is nonlinear but can be approximated by a polynomial function.

- **Evaluation Metrics**:
  - Same as Linear Regression

# 3.3 RIDGE AND LASSO REGRESSION

- **Ridge Regression**:
  - **Definition**: Ridge regression is a type of linear regression that includes a regularization term to prevent overfitting by shrinking the coefficients.
  - **Mathematical Representation**:
    $y = \beta_0 + \beta_1 x_1 + \beta_2 x_2 + \ldots + \beta_n x_n + \lambda \sum_{i=1}^{n} \beta_i^2$
    $y = \beta_0 + \beta_1 x_1 + \beta_2 x_2 + \ldots + \beta_n x_n + \lambda \sum_{i=1}^{n} \beta_i^2$
  - **Key Parameter**: Regularization parameter $\lambda$ \lambda
- **Lasso Regression**:
  - **Definition**: Lasso (Least Absolute Shrinkage and Selection Operator) regression is similar to ridge regression but uses L1 regularization, which can result in sparse models with some coefficients reduced to zero.
  - **Mathematical Representation**:
    $y = \beta_0 + \beta_1 x_1 + \beta_2 x_2 + \ldots + \beta_n x_n + \lambda \sum_{i=1}^{n} |\beta_i|$
    $y = \beta_0 + \beta_1 x_1 + \beta_2 x_2 + \ldots + \beta_n x_n + \lambda \sum_{i=1}^{n} |\beta_i|$
  - **Key Parameter**: Regularization parameter $\lambda$ \lambda

# 3.4 EVALUATION METRICS FOR REGRESSION MODELS

- **Mean Absolute Error (MAE):**
  - Definition: The average absolute difference between the predicted and actual values.
  - Formula: $MAE = \frac{1}{n} \sum_{i=1}^{n} |y_i - \hat{y_i}|$

- **Mean Squared Error (MSE):**
  - Definition: The average squared difference between the predicted and actual values.
  - Formula: $MSE = \frac{1}{n} \sum_{i=1}^{n} (y_i - \hat{y_i})^2$

- **Root Mean Squared Error (RMSE):**
  - Definition: The square root of the average squared difference between the predicted and actual values.
  - Formula: $RMSE = \sqrt{\frac{1}{n} \sum_{i=1}^{n} (y_i - \hat{y_i})^2}$

- **R-squared** ($R^2$):
  - Definition: The proportion of the variance in the target variable that is predictable from the predictor variables.
  - Formula: $R^2 = 1 - \frac{SS_{res}}{SS_{tot}}$ = 1 -

$$\frac{SS_{res}}{SS_{tot}}$$

- ○ Where $SS_{res}$ is the residual sum of squares and $SS_{tot}$ is the total sum of squares.

# TEST QUESTIONS
# AND ANSWERS

# MULTIPLE CHOICE QUESTIONS

1. **What is the primary purpose of regularization in regression models?**
   - ○ A. To increase model complexity
   - ○ B. To reduce overfitting
   - ○ C. To improve data normalization
   - ○ D. To handle missing values

**Answer:** B

2. **Which evaluation metric measures the average absolute difference between predicted and actual values?**
   - ○ A. Mean Squared Error (MSE)
   - ○ B. Root Mean Squared Error (RMSE)
   - ○ C. R-squared (R2R^2)
   - ○ D. Mean Absolute Error (MAE)

**Answer:** D

3. **In which type of regression does the relationship between the target variable and the predictor variables take the form of an nth degree polynomial?**
   - ○ A. Linear Regression
   - ○ B. Ridge Regression
   - ○ C. Polynomial Regression
   - ○ D. Lasso Regression

**Answer:** C

# TRUE OR FALSE

1. **Lasso regression uses L1 regularization, which can result in sparse models with some coefficients reduced to zero.**

**Answer**: True

2. **In linear regression, the relationship between the predictors and the target variable is assumed to be nonlinear.**

**Answer**: False

3. **Ridge regression includes a regularization term to prevent overfitting by shrinking the coefficients.**

**Answer**: True

# SHORT ANSWER QUESTIONS

1. **Explain the difference between Ridge Regression and Lasso Regression.**
   - **Answer**: Ridge regression uses L2 regularization, which penalizes the sum of the squared coefficients, while Lasso regression uses L1 regularization, which penalizes the sum of the absolute values of the coefficients. This allows Lasso to produce sparse models with some coefficients reduced to zero, effectively performing feature selection.

2. **What are the key assumptions of linear regression?**
   - **Answer**: The key assumptions of linear regression are: linearity (the relationship between predictors and the target variable is linear), independence (observations are independent of each other), homoscedasticity (the variance of the residuals is constant), and normality (the residuals are normally distributed).

3. **Name two evaluation metrics used for regression models and explain their significance.**
   - **Answer**:
     1. Mean Absolute Error (MAE): Measures the average absolute difference between the predicted and actual

values, providing a straightforward interpretation of prediction error.

2. R-squared ($R2R^2$): Indicates the proportion of the variance in the target variable that is predictable from the predictor variables, offering a measure of how well the model fits the data.

# CHAPTER 4: SUPERVISED LEARNING - CLASSIFICATION

## 4.1 Logistic Regression

- **Definition**: Logistic regression is a statistical method for analyzing a dataset in which one or more independent variables determine an outcome that is categorical.

- **Mathematical Representation**:
  - The logistic function (sigmoid function) is used to map predicted values to probabilities: $\sigma(z) = \frac{1}{1 + e^{-z}}$, where $z$ is a linear combination of the input features.
  - The output is a probability that can be thresholded to predict class labels (e.g., 0 or 1).

- **Applications**:
  - Binary classification problems such as spam detection, disease diagnosis

- **Evaluation Metrics**:
  - Accuracy
  - Precision and Recall
  - F1 Score

- Area Under the ROC Curve (AUC-ROC)

# 4.2 SUPPORT VECTOR MACHINES (SVM)

- **Definition**: Support Vector Machines are supervised learning models used for classification and regression that find the hyperplane that best separates the data into different classes.

- **Mathematical Representation**:
  - Linear SVM: $f(x)=wTx+bf(x) = w^T x + b$
  - Nonlinear SVM: Uses kernel functions (e.g., polynomial, RBF) to transform the data into a higher-dimensional space where it is linearly separable.

- **Applications**:
  - Text classification, image recognition

- **Evaluation Metrics**:
  - Same as Logistic Regression

# 4.3 DECISION TREES AND RANDOM FORESTS

- **Decision Trees**:
  - **Definition**: Decision trees are tree-structured models used for classification and regression, where internal nodes represent features, branches represent decision rules, and leaf nodes represent outcomes.
  - **Algorithm**:
    - Split the dataset based on the feature that results in the highest information gain (or lowest Gini impurity).
    - Repeat the process recursively for each subset until a stopping criterion is met.
  - **Advantages and Disadvantages**:
    - Easy to interpret and visualize
    - Prone to overfitting
- **Random Forests**:
  - **Definition**: Random forests are ensemble learning methods that create multiple decision trees during training and output the mode of the classes (classification) or mean prediction (regression) of the individual trees.
  - **Advantages and Disadvantages**:

- Reduced overfitting
- Increased accuracy
- Less interpretability compared to single decision trees

- **Evaluation Metrics:**
  - Same as Logistic Regression

# 4.4 K-NEAREST NEIGHBORS (KNN)

- **Definition**: K-Nearest Neighbors is a simple, non-parametric algorithm used for classification and regression that predicts the class of a data point based on the classes of its k nearest neighbors.
- **Algorithm**:
  - Compute the distance between the data point and all training samples.
  - Identify the k nearest neighbors.
  - Determine the class of the data point based on a majority vote (classification) or average (regression) of the neighbors' classes.
- **Distance Metrics**:
  - Euclidean distance
  - Manhattan distance
- **Applications**:
  - Pattern recognition, recommender systems
- **Evaluation Metrics**:
  - Same as Logistic Regression

# 4.5 MODEL EVALUATION METRICS

- **Accuracy**:
    - Definition: The proportion of correctly classified instances out of the total instances.
    - Formula: $\text{Accuracy} = \frac{TP + TN}{TP + TN + FP + FN}$
    - Where TP = True Positives, TN = True Negatives, FP = False Positives, FN = False Negatives
- **Precision and Recall**:
    - Precision: The proportion of true positive predictions among all positive predictions.
        - Formula: $\text{Precision} = \frac{TP}{TP + FP}$
    - Recall: The proportion of true positive predictions among all actual positives.
        - Formula: $\text{Recall} = \frac{TP}{TP + FN}$
- **F1 Score**:
    - Definition: The harmonic mean of precision and recall.
    - Formula: $\text{F1 Score} = 2 \cdot \frac{\text{Precision} \cdot \text{Recall}}{\text{Precision} + \text{Recall}}$

- **Area Under the ROC Curve (AUC-ROC):**
  - Definition: AUC-ROC measures the ability of the model to distinguish between positive and negative classes.
  - Interpretation: AUC ranges from 0 to 1, where 1 indicates perfect classification and 0.5 indicates random guessing.

# TEST QUESTIONS
# AND ANSWERS

# MULTIPLE CHOICE QUESTIONS

1. **What does the logistic function (sigmoid function) do in logistic regression?**
   - A. Maps predicted values to probabilities
   - B. Separates data into classes using a hyperplane
   - C. Constructs a decision tree
   - D. Finds the k nearest neighbors

**Answer**: A

2. **Which of the following algorithms is prone to overfitting?**
   - A. Logistic Regression
   - B. Decision Trees
   - C. Support Vector Machines (SVM)
   - D. K-Nearest Neighbors (KNN)

**Answer**: B

3. **What is the main advantage of using Random Forests over single Decision Trees?**
   - A. Easier to interpret
   - B. Increased accuracy and reduced overfitting
   - C. Requires less computational power
   - D. Better at handling categorical data

**Answer**: B

# TRUE OR FALSE

1. **Support Vector Machines (SVM) can be used for both classification and regression tasks.**

**Answer**: True

2. **K-Nearest Neighbors (KNN) is a parametric algorithm.**

**Answer**: False

3. **Precision measures the proportion of true positive predictions among all actual positives.**

**Answer**: False (Precision measures the proportion of true positive predictions among all positive predictions)

# SHORT ANSWER QUESTIONS

1. **Explain the difference between precision and recall.**
   - **Answer**: Precision is the proportion of true positive predictions among all positive predictions, while recall is the proportion of true positive predictions among all actual positives. Precision focuses on the accuracy of positive predictions, whereas recall focuses on capturing all actual positives.

2. **What is the purpose of the kernel function in Support Vector Machines (SVM)?**
   - **Answer**: The kernel function in SVM is used to transform the data into a higher-dimensional space where it becomes linearly separable, allowing the algorithm to create an optimal hyperplane for classification.

3. **List two evaluation metrics commonly used for classification models and explain their significance.**
   - **Answer**:
     1. Accuracy: Measures the proportion of correctly classified instances out of the total instances, providing an overall measure of model performance.
     2. F1 Score: The harmonic mean of precision and recall, balancing the trade-off between precision and recall,

and useful when dealing with imbalanced datasets.

# CHAPTER 5: UNSUPERVISED LEARNING

## 5.1 Clustering Algorithms

Clustering algorithms are used to group a set of objects in such a way that objects in the same group (or cluster) are more similar to each other than to those in other groups.

### 5.1.1 K-Means Clustering

- **Definition**: K-Means clustering partitions the data into K clusters where each data point belongs to the cluster with the nearest mean.

- **Algorithm**:
  - Initialize K centroids randomly.
  - Assign each data point to the nearest centroid.
  - Update centroids by calculating the mean of assigned points.
  - Repeat the assignment and update steps until convergence.

- **Evaluation Metrics**:
  - Elbow Method
  - Silhouette Score

### 5.1.2 Hierarchical Clustering

- **Definition**: Hierarchical clustering builds a tree-like structure of clusters by either iteratively merging smaller clusters (agglomerative) or splitting larger clusters (divisive).

- **Algorithm (Agglomerative)**:
  - Start with each data point as its own cluster.
  - Merge the two closest clusters.
  - Repeat until all points are in a single cluster.
- **Dendrogram**: A visual representation of the hierarchical structure.
- **Evaluation Metrics**:
  - Cophenetic Correlation Coefficient

### 5.1.3 DBSCAN (Density-Based Spatial Clustering of Applications with Noise)

- **Definition**: DBSCAN groups together points that are closely packed together, marking points in low-density regions as outliers.
- **Algorithm**:
  - Define a neighborhood for each point.
  - Classify points as core, border, or noise.
  - Expand clusters from core points.
- **Advantages**:
  - Can find arbitrarily shaped clusters.
  - Robust to outliers.

# 5.2 DIMENSIONALITY REDUCTION TECHNIQUES

Dimensionality reduction is the process of reducing the number of random variables under consideration by obtaining a set of principal variables.

*5.2.1 Principal Component Analysis (PCA)*

- **Definition**: PCA is a statistical technique that transforms data into a new coordinate system, where the greatest variance lies on the first principal component, the second greatest variance on the second, and so on.

- **Algorithm**:
  - Standardize the data.
  - Compute the covariance matrix.
  - Calculate eigenvalues and eigenvectors.
  - Sort eigenvectors by eigenvalues in descending order.
  - Transform the data.

*5.2.2 Linear Discriminant Analysis (LDA)*

- **Definition**: LDA is used to find a linear combination of features that characterizes or separates two or more classes.

- **Applications**:

○ Classification tasks

### 5.2.3 t-Distributed Stochastic Neighbor Embedding (t-SNE)

- **Definition**: t-SNE is a nonlinear dimensionality reduction technique that is particularly well suited for embedding high-dimensional data into a two or three-dimensional space for visualization.

- **Algorithm**:

  ○ Compute pairwise similarities in high-dimensional space.

  ○ Compute pairwise similarities in low-dimensional space.

  ○ Minimize the difference between these similarities.

# 5.3 ANOMALY DETECTION

Anomaly detection is the identification of rare items, events, or observations which raise suspicions by differing significantly from the majority of the data.

*Techniques:*

- **Statistical Methods**: Z-score, Grubbs' test
- **Machine Learning Methods**: Isolation Forest, One-Class SVM
- **Applications**:
  - Fraud detection, Network security

# 5.4 ASSOCIATION RULE LEARNING

Association rule learning is a rule-based machine learning method for discovering interesting relations between variables in large databases.

### 5.4.1 Apriori Algorithm

- **Definition**: Apriori is an algorithm for frequent item set mining and association rule learning over transactional databases.
- **Algorithm**:
    - Identify frequent individual items.
    - Extend them to larger item sets as long as those item sets appear sufficiently often in the database.

### 5.4.2 Eclat Algorithm

- **Definition**: Eclat (Equivalence Class Clustering and bottom-up Lattice Traversal) is an algorithm for mining frequent item sets using a depth-first search strategy.
- **Comparison with Apriori**:
    - Eclat is typically faster as it uses vertical data format.

# TEST QUESTIONS
# AND ANSWERS

# MULTIPLE CHOICE QUESTIONS

1. **What is the main purpose of clustering algorithms?**
   - A. To predict target variables
   - B. To group similar data points
   - C. To reduce dimensionality
   - D. To detect anomalies

**Answer:** B

2. **Which of the following algorithms can find arbitrarily shaped clusters and is robust to outliers?**
   - A. K-Means Clustering
   - B. Hierarchical Clustering
   - C. DBSCAN
   - D. PCA

**Answer:** C

3. **What technique does t-SNE use for dimensionality reduction?**
   - A. Linear transformation
   - B. Nonlinear embedding
   - C. Covariance matrix
   - D. Depth-first search

**Answer:** B

# TRUE OR FALSE

1. **Principal Component Analysis (PCA) can reduce the number of variables while preserving as much variability as possible.**

**Answer**: True

2. **The Apriori algorithm uses a breadth-first search strategy for mining frequent item sets.**

**Answer**: True

3. **Isolation Forest is a technique used for anomaly detection.**

**Answer**: True

# SHORT ANSWER QUESTIONS

1. **Explain the difference between agglomerative and divisive hierarchical clustering.**

   - **Answer**: Agglomerative hierarchical clustering starts with each data point as its own cluster and iteratively merges the closest clusters until all points are in a single cluster. Divisive hierarchical clustering, on the other hand, starts with all points in a single cluster and iteratively splits the clusters until each data point is its own cluster.

2. **What is the main advantage of using DBSCAN over K-Means clustering?**

   - **Answer**: The main advantage of DBSCAN over K-Means clustering is that DBSCAN can find arbitrarily shaped clusters and is robust to outliers, whereas K-Means clustering assumes spherical clusters and is sensitive to outliers.

3. **Describe a real-world application of anomaly detection.**

   - **Answer**: A real-world application of anomaly detection is fraud detection in financial transactions. By identifying transactions that deviate significantly from normal behavior, anomaly detection algorithms can help detect and prevent fraudulent activities.

# CHAPTER 6: NEURAL NETWORKS AND DEEP LEARNING

## 6.1 Introduction to Neural Networks

- **Definition**: Neural networks are computational models inspired by the human brain, consisting of interconnected nodes (neurons) organized in layers.

- **Architecture**:
  - **Input Layer**: Receives input data.
  - **Hidden Layers**: Perform computations and extract features.
  - **Output Layer**: Produces the final output.

- **Activation Functions**:
  - **Sigmoid**: $\sigma(x) = \frac{1}{1 + e^{-x}}$
  - **ReLU (Rectified Linear Unit)**: $\text{ReLU}(x) = \max(0, x)$
  - **Tanh**: $\tanh(x) = \frac{e^x - e^{-x}}{e^x + e^{-x}}$

- **Training Process**:
  - **Forward Propagation**: Pass input through the network to get output.
  - **Loss Function**: Measure the difference between predicted and actual output.

- **Backward Propagation**: Update weights to minimize the loss.

# 6.2 CONVOLUTIONAL NEURAL NETWORKS (CNNS)

- **Definition**: CNNs are a class of neural networks specifically designed for processing structured grid data such as images.
- **Architecture**:
  - **Convolutional Layers**: Apply convolution operations to extract features.
  - **Pooling Layers**: Reduce dimensionality while retaining important information.
  - **Fully Connected Layers**: Connect every neuron in one layer to every neuron in the next.
- **Applications**:
  - Image classification, object detection, facial recognition

# 6.3 RECURRENT NEURAL NETWORKS (RNNS) AND LSTMS

- **Definition**: RNNs are a class of neural networks designed to handle sequential data by maintaining a hidden state that captures information from previous time steps.
- **Limitations of RNNs**:
  - Difficulty in learning long-term dependencies
  - Vanishing gradient problem
- **LSTMs (Long Short-Term Memory)**:
  - **Definition**: LSTMs are a type of RNN designed to overcome the limitations of traditional RNNs by introducing memory cells that can maintain information over long periods.
  - **Components**:
    - Forget Gate: Decides what information to discard.
    - Input Gate: Decides what information to store.
    - Output Gate: Decides what information to output.
- **Applications**:
  - Natural language processing (NLP), time series prediction, speech recognition

# 6.4 DEEP LEARNING FRAMEWORKS

- **TensorFlow**:
  - Developed by Google.
  - Provides a comprehensive ecosystem for building and deploying machine learning models.
- **Keras**:
  - High-level neural networks API written in Python.
  - Runs on top of TensorFlow and other frameworks.
  - Simplifies the process of building neural networks.
- **PyTorch**:
  - Developed by Facebook's AI Research lab (FAIR).
  - Known for its dynamic computational graph and ease of use.
  - Popular for research and prototyping.

# 6.5 PRACTICAL CONSIDERATIONS

- **Data Preparation**:
    - Normalize data to a consistent scale.
    - Augment data to increase diversity and robustness.
- **Model Training**:
    - Split data into training, validation, and test sets.
    - Use techniques like early stopping and dropout to prevent overfitting.
- **Model Evaluation**:
    - Monitor metrics such as accuracy, precision, recall, and loss.
    - Use confusion matrix and ROC curves for classification tasks.

# TEST QUESTIONS
# AND ANSWERS

# MULTIPLE CHOICE QUESTIONS

1. **What is the primary purpose of the activation function in a neural network?**
   - A. To initialize the weights
   - B. To transform the input data
   - C. To introduce non-linearity into the model
   - D. To reduce dimensionality

**Answer**: C

2. **Which of the following is a common activation function used in neural networks?**
   - A. Logistic function
   - B. Convolutional function
   - C. Pooling function
   - D. Sigmoid function

**Answer**: D

3. **What problem do LSTM networks address in traditional RNNs?**
   - A. Overfitting
   - B. Long-term dependency and vanishing gradient problems
   - C. Lack of non-linearity
   - D. Dimensionality reduction

**Answer**: B

# TRUE OR FALSE

1. **Convolutional Neural Networks (CNNs) are specifically designed for processing sequential data.**

**Answer**: False (CNNs are designed for processing structured grid data like images)

2. **PyTorch is known for its dynamic computational graph and ease of use, making it popular for research and prototyping.**

**Answer**: True

3. **The output layer of a neural network is responsible for producing the final output.**

**Answer**: True

# SHORT ANSWER QUESTIONS

1. **What are the key components of an LSTM network, and what are their functions?**

    - **Answer**: The key components of an LSTM network are:

        1. Forget Gate: Decides what information to discard from the cell state.

        2. Input Gate: Decides what information to store in the cell state.

        3. Output Gate: Decides what information to output from the cell state.

2. **Explain the difference between TensorFlow and Keras.**

    - **Answer**: TensorFlow is a comprehensive ecosystem for building and deploying machine learning models, developed by Google. Keras is a high-level neural networks API written in Python that runs on top of TensorFlow (and other frameworks). Keras simplifies the process of building neural networks by providing an easy-to-use interface.

3. **Describe a real-world application of Convolutional Neural Networks (CNNs).**

    - **Answer**: A real-world application of Convolutional Neural Networks (CNNs) is image classification. CNNs can be used to classify images into different categories, such as identifying objects in photos, recognizing facial expressions, and detecting abnormalities in medical images.

# CHAPTER 7: REINFORCEMENT LEARNING

## 7.1 Fundamentals of Reinforcement Learning

- **Definition**: Reinforcement learning (RL) is a type of machine learning where an agent learns to make decisions by taking actions in an environment to maximize cumulative reward.

- **Key Components**:
  - **Agent**: The learner or decision-maker.
  - **Environment**: The world with which the agent interacts.
  - **State**: A representation of the current situation.
  - **Action**: Choices made by the agent.
  - **Reward**: Feedback from the environment to evaluate actions.
  - **Policy**: The strategy used by the agent to decide actions.
  - **Value Function**: Estimates the expected cumulative reward for states or state-action pairs.

# 7.2 MARKOV DECISION PROCESSES (MDPS)

- **Definition**: MDPs provide a mathematical framework for modeling decision-making situations where outcomes are partly random and partly under the control of the agent.

- **Components of MDPs**:
    - **States (S)**: The set of all possible states.
    - **Actions (A)**: The set of all possible actions.
    - **Transition Function (P)**: The probability of transitioning from one state to another given an action.
    - **Reward Function (R)**: The immediate reward received after transitioning from one state to another.
    - **Discount Factor (γ)**: A factor between 0 and 1 that discounts future rewards.

# 7.3 Q-LEARNING AND SARSA

- **Q-Learning**:
  - **Definition**: Q-Learning is an off-policy RL algorithm that learns the value of an action in a particular state.
  - **Q-Value (Q-function)**: Represents the expected cumulative reward of taking an action in a state and following the optimal policy thereafter.
  - **Update Rule**: $Q(s,a) \leftarrow Q(s,a) + \alpha[r + \gamma \max_{a'} Q(s', a') - Q(s, a)]$
  - **Exploration vs. Exploitation**: Balancing between exploring new actions and exploiting known actions to maximize reward.
- **SARSA (State-Action-Reward-State-Action)**:
  - **Definition**: SARSA is an on-policy RL algorithm that updates the Q-values based on the action actually taken by the current policy.
  - **Update Rule**: $Q(s,a) \leftarrow Q(s,a) + \alpha[r + \gamma Q(s', a') - Q(s, a)]$

# 7.4 DEEP REINFORCEMENT LEARNING

- **Definition**: Deep reinforcement learning combines deep learning with reinforcement learning to solve complex problems with high-dimensional state and action spaces.

- **Deep Q-Networks (DQNs)**:
  - **Definition**: Uses deep neural networks to approximate Q-values for all actions in a given state.
  - **Experience Replay**: Stores and reuses past experiences to stabilize training.
  - **Target Network**: A separate network used to compute target Q-values to reduce oscillations and divergence during training.

# 7.5 APPLICATIONS OF REINFORCEMENT LEARNING

- **Game Playing**: RL has been used to create agents that can play and excel at various games, such as Chess, Go, and video games (e.g., DeepMind's AlphaGo).
- **Robotics**: RL is used to teach robots to perform tasks such as walking, grasping, and navigating.
- **Finance**: RL algorithms are applied to optimize trading strategies and portfolio management.
- **Healthcare**: RL can assist in personalized treatment planning and drug discovery.

# TEST QUESTIONS
# AND ANSWERS

# MULTIPLE CHOICE QUESTIONS

1. **What is the main goal of an agent in reinforcement learning?**
   - ◦ A. To classify data
   - ◦ B. To minimize cumulative reward
   - ◦ C. To maximize cumulative reward
   - ◦ D. To reduce dimensionality

**Answer:** C

2. **What does the discount factor (γ) in Markov Decision Processes represent?**
   - ◦ A. The probability of transitioning from one state to another
   - ◦ B. The immediate reward received after an action
   - ◦ C. The factor that discounts future rewards
   - ◦ D. The strategy used by the agent to decide actions

**Answer:** C

3. **Which algorithm uses a separate network to compute target Q-values to reduce oscillations and divergence during training?**
   - ◦ A. SARSA
   - ◦ B. Q-Learning
   - ◦ C. Deep Q-Networks (DQNs)

- ◦ D. Markov Decision Processes (MDPs)

**Answer**: C

# TRUE OR FALSE

1. **In Q-Learning, the Q-values are updated based on the action actually taken by the current policy.**

**Answer**: False (Q-Learning is an off-policy algorithm that updates Q-values based on the maximum future reward)

2. **Experience replay is a technique used in Deep Q-Networks (DQNs) to store and reuse past experiences.**

**Answer**: True

3. **Reinforcement learning can be applied to healthcare for personalized treatment planning.**

**Answer**: True

# SHORT ANSWER QUESTIONS

1. **Explain the difference between Q-Learning and SARSA.**
   - **Answer**: Q-Learning is an off-policy algorithm that updates Q-values based on the maximum future reward, regardless of the action actually taken. SARSA is an on-policy algorithm that updates Q-values based on the action taken by the current policy.

2. **What is the purpose of using a target network in Deep Q-Networks (DQNs)?**
   - **Answer**: The target network in Deep Q-Networks (DQNs) is used to compute target Q-values, which helps reduce oscillations and divergence during training by providing a more stable target for updates.

3. **Describe a real-world application of reinforcement learning in robotics.**
   - **Answer**: A real-world application of reinforcement learning in robotics is teaching a robot to navigate an environment autonomously. RL algorithms can be used to train the robot to make decisions and take actions that maximize its ability to reach a target location while avoiding obstacles.

# CHAPTER 8: MODEL SELECTION AND OPTIMIZATION

## 8.1 Cross-Validation Techniques

Cross-validation is a technique used to assess the performance of a machine learning model by dividing the data into subsets and evaluating the model on different subsets.

### 8.1.1 K-Fold Cross-Validation

- **Definition**: K-Fold Cross-Validation splits the data into K equal-sized folds. The model is trained on K-1 folds and tested on the remaining fold. This process is repeated K times, each time with a different fold as the test set.
- **Algorithm**:
  - Divide the dataset into K folds.
  - For each fold:
    - Train the model on K-1 folds.
    - Test the model on the remaining fold.
  - Compute the average performance across all K iterations.
- **Advantages**:
  - More reliable estimate of model performance.
  - Reduces the impact of data partitioning.

### 8.1.2 Leave-One-Out Cross-Validation (LOOCV)

- **Definition**: LOOCV is a special case of K-Fold Cross-

Validation where K is equal to the number of data points. Each data point is used once as the test set while the remaining points are used for training.

- **Advantages**:
  - Provides the most accurate estimate of model performance.
- **Disadvantages**:
  - Computationally expensive for large datasets.

### 8.1.3 Stratified Cross-Validation

- **Definition**: Stratified Cross-Validation ensures that the folds are representative of the original dataset's class distribution. It is commonly used in classification tasks.
- **Algorithm**:
  - Divide the dataset into K folds while maintaining the class distribution.
  - Apply the same process as K-Fold Cross-Validation.

# 8.2 HYPERPARAMETER TUNING

Hyperparameter tuning involves finding the best hyperparameters for a machine learning model to optimize its performance.

### 8.2.1 Grid Search

- **Definition**: Grid Search exhaustively searches through a specified subset of hyperparameters to find the best combination.
- **Algorithm**:
  - Define a grid of hyperparameters.
  - Train the model for each combination of hyperparameters.
  - Evaluate the model's performance and select the best combination.
- **Advantages**:
  - Simple to implement.
- **Disadvantages**:
  - Computationally expensive.

### 8.2.2 Random Search

- **Definition**: Random Search selects random combinations of hyperparameters from a specified subset and evaluates the model's performance.
- **Algorithm**:
  - Define a range of hyperparameters.

- Randomly sample combinations of hyperparameters.
- Train and evaluate the model for each combination.
- Select the best combination.

- **Advantages**:
  - More efficient than Grid Search.
- **Disadvantages**:
  - May not find the optimal combination.

# 8.3 MODEL ENSEMBLE TECHNIQUES

Model ensembling combines multiple models to improve overall performance and reduce the risk of overfitting.

### 8.3.1 Bagging (Bootstrap Aggregating)

- **Definition**: Bagging reduces variance by training multiple models on different bootstrap samples of the data and averaging their predictions.
- **Algorithm**:
  - Create multiple bootstrap samples from the training data.
  - Train a model on each sample.
  - Aggregate the predictions (e.g., by voting for classification or averaging for regression).
- **Example**: Random Forests.

### 8.3.2 Boosting

- **Definition**: Boosting reduces bias by sequentially training models, where each model corrects the errors of the previous one.
- **Algorithm**:
  - Initialize weights for each data point.
  - Train a model and evaluate its performance.
  - Increase the weights of misclassified points and decrease the weights of correctly classified points.

- Repeat the process with the adjusted weights.
- **Example**: AdaBoost, Gradient Boosting.

### 8.3.3 Stacking

- **Definition**: Stacking combines the predictions of multiple base models to create a meta-model that improves overall performance.
- **Algorithm**:
  - Train multiple base models on the training data.
  - Use the predictions of the base models as input features for the meta-model.
  - Train the meta-model to make the final predictions.

# TEST QUESTIONS
# AND ANSWERS

# MULTIPLE CHOICE QUESTIONS

1. **What is the primary purpose of cross-validation?**
   - A. To increase model complexity
   - B. To estimate model performance
   - C. To reduce dimensionality
   - D. To handle missing values

**Answer:** B

2. **Which hyperparameter tuning technique exhaustively searches through a specified subset of hyperparameters?**
   - A. Random Search
   - B. Grid Search
   - C. Stacking
   - D. Bagging

**Answer:** B

3. **What is the main advantage of using Random Search over Grid Search?**
   - A. Less computationally expensive
   - B. More likely to find the optimal combination
   - C. More accurate
   - D. Easier to interpret

**Answer:** A

# TRUE OR FALSE

1. **Stratified Cross-Validation ensures that the folds are representative of the original dataset's class distribution.**

**Answer:** True

2. **Bagging reduces bias by sequentially training models where each model corrects the errors of the previous one.**

**Answer:** False (Bagging reduces variance, not bias)

3. **Stacking combines the predictions of multiple base models to create a meta-model that improves overall performance.**

**Answer:** True

# SHORT ANSWER QUESTIONS

1. **Explain the difference between Bagging and Boosting.**
   - **Answer**: Bagging reduces variance by training multiple models on different bootstrap samples of the data and averaging their predictions. Boosting reduces bias by sequentially training models, where each model corrects the errors of the previous one.

2. **What is the purpose of hyperparameter tuning in machine learning?**
   - **Answer**: The purpose of hyperparameter tuning is to find the best hyperparameters for a machine learning model to optimize its performance and achieve better results.

3. **Describe a real-world application of model ensembling.**
   - **Answer**: A real-world application of model ensembling is in medical diagnostics. By combining the predictions of multiple models, ensemble methods can improve the accuracy and reliability of diagnosing diseases, leading to better patient outcomes.

# CHAPTER 9: MODEL DEPLOYMENT AND MAINTENANCE

## 9.1 Model Deployment Strategies

Model deployment is the process of integrating a machine learning model into a production environment where it can be used to make predictions on new data.

### 9.1.1 Batch Deployment

- **Definition**: Batch deployment involves running the model on a batch of data at scheduled intervals.
- **Advantages**:
  - Suitable for large datasets.
  - Can process data in bulk, leading to efficient use of resources.
- **Disadvantages**:
  - Delayed predictions due to scheduled intervals.
  - Not suitable for real-time applications.

### 9.1.2 Online Deployment

- **Definition**: Online deployment involves serving the model to make predictions in real-time as new data comes in.
- **Advantages**:
  - Provides instant predictions.
  - Suitable for real-time applications.

- **Disadvantages**:
    - Requires robust infrastructure.
    - Higher operational costs.

# 9.2 MONITORING AND MAINTAINING MODELS IN PRODUCTION

Once a model is deployed, it is essential to continuously monitor and maintain it to ensure it performs as expected.

### 9.2.1 Monitoring

- **Definition**: Monitoring involves tracking the model's performance and behavior in the production environment.
- **Metrics to Monitor**:
  - Prediction accuracy
  - Latency
  - Resource usage (CPU, memory)
  - Data drift
- **Tools for Monitoring**:
  - Prometheus
  - Grafana
  - ELK Stack (Elasticsearch, Logstash, Kibana)

### 9.2.2 Maintenance

- **Definition**: Maintenance involves updating the model and infrastructure to adapt to changes and maintain optimal performance.
- **Strategies for Maintenance**:
  - Regular retraining with new data.

- Hyperparameter tuning to adapt to changes.
- Updating the model architecture if necessary.
- Ensuring the infrastructure is scalable and resilient.

# 9.3 A/B TESTING AND MODEL PERFORMANCE TRACKING

A/B testing is a method used to compare the performance of two models (or model versions) to determine which one performs better.

### 9.3.1 A/B Testing

- **Definition**: A/B testing involves deploying two versions of a model (A and B) and comparing their performance on different subsets of data.

- **Steps in A/B Testing**:
  - Define the metrics to evaluate.
  - Split the traffic between the two models.
  - Collect and analyze the results.
  - Determine the better performing model.

- **Advantages**:
  - Provides a controlled environment to test model changes.
  - Helps in making data-driven decisions.

### 9.3.2 Model Performance Tracking

- **Definition**: Model performance tracking involves keeping a record of the model's performance metrics over time to identify trends and anomalies.

- **Tools for Performance Tracking**:
  - MLflow
  - TensorBoard
  - Neptune.ai
- **Metrics to Track**:
  - Accuracy, precision, recall, F1 score
  - ROC-AUC
  - Latency
  - Resource usage

# 9.4 HANDLING MODEL DRIFT AND RETRAINING

Model drift occurs when the model's performance degrades over time due to changes in the data or environment.

### 9.4.1 Types of Model Drift

- **Data Drift**: Changes in the input data distribution.
- **Concept Drift**: Changes in the relationship between input data and target variable.

### 9.4.2 Detecting and Handling Model Drift

- **Detection Methods**:
  - Monitor performance metrics.
  - Statistical tests (e.g., Kolmogorov-Smirnov test).
- **Handling Model Drift**:
  - Retrain the model with updated data.
  - Use adaptive algorithms that can adjust to changes.
  - Implement continuous monitoring and automated retraining pipelines.

# TEST QUESTIONS
# AND ANSWERS

# MULTIPLE CHOICE QUESTIONS

1. **What is the main advantage of online deployment over batch deployment?**
   - A. Suitable for large datasets
   - B. Provides instant predictions
   - C. Requires less infrastructure
   - D. Lower operational costs

**Answer:** B

2. **Which tool is commonly used for monitoring model performance and behavior in production?**
   - A. TensorBoard
   - B. Grafana
   - C. MLflow
   - D. Jupyter Notebook

**Answer:** B

3. **What is the purpose of A/B testing in model deployment?**
   - A. To process data in bulk
   - B. To reduce operational costs
   - C. To compare the performance of two models
   - D. To implement continuous monitoring

**Answer:** C

# TRUE OR FALSE

1. **Batch deployment involves serving the model to make predictions in real-time as new data comes in.**

**Answer**: False (Batch deployment processes data at scheduled intervals)

2. **Model drift occurs when the model's performance improves over time due to changes in the data or environment.**

**Answer**: False (Model drift occurs when the model's performance degrades over time)

3. **A/B testing provides a controlled environment to test model changes and helps in making data-driven decisions.**

**Answer**: True

# SHORT ANSWER QUESTIONS

1. **What is the difference between data drift and concept drift?**

   - **Answer**: Data drift refers to changes in the input data distribution, while concept drift refers to changes in the relationship between input data and the target variable.

2. **List two metrics that should be monitored to track a model's performance in production.**

   - **Answer**:

     1. Prediction accuracy
     2. Latency

3. **Describe a strategy to handle model drift.**

   - **Answer**: One strategy to handle model drift is to regularly retrain the model with updated data to ensure it adapts to changes in the data or environment. This can be implemented through continuous monitoring and automated retraining pipelines.

# CHAPTER 10: ETHICAL AND RESPONSIBLE AI

## 10.1 Fairness and Bias in Machine Learning

- **Definition**: Fairness in machine learning ensures that models do not exhibit bias or discriminate against any individuals or groups.
- **Sources of Bias**:
    - **Data Collection**: Biases in the data used for training can lead to biased models.
    - **Feature Selection**: Including biased features can result in biased predictions.
    - **Model Training**: Biases can be introduced during the model training process.
- **Types of Bias**:
    - **Algorithmic Bias**: Biases introduced by the machine learning algorithms themselves.
    - **Human Bias**: Biases introduced by human decisions and actions.
- **Mitigation Techniques**:
    - **Data Preprocessing**: Addressing biases in the training data.
    - **Fairness Constraints**: Applying constraints during model training.
    - **Post-processing**: Adjusting model outputs to reduce bias.
- **Examples**:

- Ensuring non-discriminatory hiring practices.
- Preventing biased credit scoring.

# 10.2 PRIVACY AND SECURITY CONCERNS

- **Data Privacy**:
  - **Definition**: Protecting individuals' personal data from unauthorized access and use.
  - **Techniques**:
    - **Data Anonymization**: Removing personally identifiable information.
    - **Differential Privacy**: Adding noise to data to prevent re-identification.
- **Data Security**:
  - **Definition**: Ensuring the integrity, confidentiality, and availability of data.
  - **Techniques**:
    - **Encryption**: Protecting data during storage and transmission.
    - **Access Control**: Restricting access to sensitive data.
- **Regulations**:
  - **GDPR (General Data Protection Regulation)**: European regulation on data protection and privacy.
  - **CCPA (California Consumer Privacy Act)**: California regulation on consumer data privacy.

# 10.3 INTERPRETABLE MACHINE LEARNING

- **Definition**: Interpretable machine learning ensures that the decisions made by models can be understood and explained by humans.
- **Importance**:
    - **Trust**: Building trust in AI systems.
    - **Accountability**: Ensuring accountability for decisions made by AI.
    - **Compliance**: Meeting regulatory requirements.
- **Techniques for Interpretability**:
    - **Feature Importance**: Identifying which features have the most influence on predictions.
    - **SHAP (SHapley Additive exPlanations)**: Explaining the contribution of each feature to the prediction.
    - **LIME (Local Interpretable Model-agnostic Explanations)**: Providing local explanations for individual predictions.
- **Examples**:
    - Explaining loan approval decisions.
    - Interpreting medical diagnosis predictions.

# 10.4 REGULATIONS AND COMPLIANCE

- **Global Regulations**:
    - **GDPR**: Protects data privacy and provides individuals with rights over their data.
    - **CCPA**: Provides California residents with rights regarding their personal information.
- **Compliance Requirements**:
    - **Data Protection Impact Assessments (DPIAs)**: Assessing the impact of data processing activities on privacy.
    - **Record Keeping**: Maintaining records of data processing activities.
    - **Rights of Data Subjects**: Ensuring individuals can exercise their rights, such as the right to access, rectify, and delete their data.
- **Ethical Guidelines**:
    - **Principles of Beneficence and Non-Maleficence**: Ensuring AI systems benefit society and do not cause harm.
    - **Transparency**: Being open about how AI systems operate and make decisions.
    - **Inclusiveness**: Ensuring AI systems are designed and used in an inclusive manner.

# TEST QUESTIONS
# AND ANSWERS

# MULTIPLE CHOICE QUESTIONS

1. **What is the primary purpose of fairness in machine learning?**
   - ◦ A. To increase model complexity
   - ◦ B. To ensure models do not exhibit bias or discrimination
   - ◦ C. To reduce dimensionality
   - ◦ D. To handle missing values

**Answer**: B

2. **Which regulation provides European citizens with rights over their personal data?**
   - ◦ A. CCPA
   - ◦ B. HIPAA
   - ◦ C. GDPR
   - ◦ D. FERPA

**Answer**: C

3. **What is the purpose of data anonymization?**
   - ◦ A. To increase model accuracy
   - ◦ B. To remove personally identifiable information
   - ◦ C. To optimize hyperparameters
   - ◦ D. To visualize data

**Answer**: B

# TRUE OR FALSE

1. **Differential privacy adds noise to data to prevent re-identification.**

**Answer**: True

2. **SHAP (SHapley Additive exPlanations) provides local explanations for individual predictions.**

**Answer**: False (SHAP explains the contribution of each feature to the prediction)

3. **GDPR is a regulation that provides California residents with rights regarding their personal information.**

**Answer**: False (GDPR applies to European citizens, while CCPA applies to California residents)

# SHORT ANSWER QUESTIONS

1. **What is the difference between data privacy and data security?**
   - **Answer**: Data privacy focuses on protecting individuals' personal data from unauthorized access and use, while data security ensures the integrity, confidentiality, and availability of data.

2. **Name two techniques used to improve the interpretability of machine learning models.**
   - **Answer**:
     1. SHAP (SHapley Additive exPlanations)
     2. LIME (Local Interpretable Model-agnostic Explanations)

3. **Describe a real-world application of fairness in machine learning.**
   - **Answer**: A real-world application of fairness in machine learning is ensuring non-discriminatory hiring practices. By using fair and unbiased models, companies can prevent discrimination based on race, gender, or other protected characteristics when making hiring decisions.

# CHAPTER 11: CAPSTONE PROJECT

## 11.1 Project Selection and Planning

- **Definition**: The capstone project is a comprehensive project that allows students to apply the knowledge and skills they have acquired throughout the course to solve a real-world problem using machine learning.

- **Choosing a Project**:
  - **Relevance**: Select a project that aligns with your interests and career goals.
  - **Feasibility**: Ensure that the project is achievable within the given time frame and resources.
  - **Impact**: Choose a project that has the potential to make a meaningful contribution or solve a significant problem.

- **Project Proposal**:
  - **Problem Statement**: Clearly define the problem you aim to solve.
  - **Objectives**: Outline the goals and expected outcomes of the project.
  - **Methodology**: Describe the approach and techniques you plan to use.
  - **Timeline**: Create a detailed timeline with milestones and deadlines.

# 11.2 DATA COLLECTION AND PREPROCESSING

- **Data Collection**:
    - **Sources**: Identify and gather relevant data from various sources (e.g., public datasets, APIs, web scraping).
    - **Data Privacy**: Ensure that data collection complies with privacy and ethical guidelines.
- **Data Preprocessing**:
    - **Cleaning**: Handle missing values, remove duplicates, and address outliers.
    - **Transformation**: Normalize, standardize, and encode features as needed.
    - **Exploration**: Perform exploratory data analysis (EDA) to understand the data and identify patterns.

# 11.3 MODEL DEVELOPMENT AND EVALUATION

- **Model Selection**:
  - **Algorithms**: Choose appropriate machine learning algorithms based on the problem type (e.g., classification, regression, clustering).
  - **Baseline Model**: Start with a simple baseline model to set a performance benchmark.
- **Model Training**:
  - **Training Set**: Split the data into training, validation, and test sets.
  - **Hyperparameter Tuning**: Use techniques like grid search or random search to find the best hyperparameters.
  - **Cross-Validation**: Apply cross-validation techniques to ensure robust model performance.
- **Model Evaluation**:
  - **Metrics**: Evaluate the model using relevant metrics (e.g., accuracy, precision, recall, F1 score, ROC-AUC).
  - **Model Comparison**: Compare the performance of different models and select the best one.
  - **Error Analysis**: Analyze the model's errors to

identify areas for improvement.

# 11.4 DEPLOYMENT AND PRESENTATION

- **Model Deployment**:
    - **Deployment Strategies**: Choose between batch deployment and online deployment based on the project's requirements.
    - **Integration**: Integrate the model into a production environment or application.
    - **Monitoring**: Set up monitoring to track the model's performance and behavior in production.
- **Project Presentation**:
    - **Report**: Prepare a comprehensive report detailing the project's objectives, methodology, results, and conclusions.
    - **Visualization**: Create visualizations to effectively communicate findings and insights.
    - **Presentation**: Present the project to an audience, highlighting key aspects and answering questions.

# 11.5 REFLECTIONS AND FUTURE WORK

- **Reflections**:
    - **Challenges**: Reflect on the challenges faced during the project and how they were addressed.
    - **Learnings**: Summarize the key learnings and insights gained from the project.
- **Future Work**:
    - **Improvements**: Identify areas for improvement and potential enhancements to the model.
    - **Extensions**: Suggest future projects or research that build on the current work.

# TEST QUESTIONS
# AND ANSWERS

# MULTIPLE CHOICE QUESTIONS

1. **What should be the primary consideration when selecting a capstone project?**
   - A. The project's alignment with course material
   - B. The project's feasibility within the given time frame
   - C. The potential impact of the project
   - D. All of the above

**Answer:** D

2. **Which of the following is NOT a typical step in data preprocessing?**
   - A. Data cleaning
   - B. Data exploration
   - C. Data encryption
   - D. Data transformation

**Answer:** C

3. **What is the purpose of hyperparameter tuning in model development?**
   - A. To clean the data
   - B. To optimize model performance
   - C. To deploy the model
   - D. To collect the data

**Answer:** B

# TRUE OR FALSE

1. **A baseline model is used to set a performance benchmark for comparison.**

**Answer**: True

2. **Model deployment involves only batch processing of data.**

**Answer**: False (Model deployment can involve both batch and online processing)

3. **Cross-validation is used to ensure robust model performance.**

**Answer**: True

# SHORT ANSWER QUESTIONS

1. **What is the significance of error analysis in model evaluation?**
   - **Answer**: Error analysis helps identify the areas where the model performs poorly and provides insights into potential improvements. It enables understanding of the model's limitations and guides further refinement.

2. **Name two key components that should be included in the project proposal for a capstone project.**
   - **Answer**:
     1. Problem Statement
     2. Objectives

3. **Describe a real-world scenario where model deployment would be critical.**
   - **Answer**: A real-world scenario where model deployment would be critical is in healthcare, where a predictive model can be deployed to assist doctors in diagnosing diseases based on patient data. Real-time deployment would enable instant predictions and support timely decision-making for patient care.

# ACKNOWLEDGEMENT

Creating **"Machine Learning - Complete Crash Course with Test Q&A"** has been a remarkable journey, and it wouldn't have been possible without the support and contributions of many individuals and organizations.

First and foremost, I would like to express my heartfelt gratitude to **Microsoft** for providing the incredible platform and tools that empowered me to compile and present this comprehensive guide. Their commitment to advancing artificial intelligence and machine learning has been truly inspiring.

I am immensely grateful to the **researchers, engineers, and educators** in the field of machine learning whose groundbreaking work and insights have paved the way for this book. Their dedication to knowledge and innovation continues to push the boundaries of what is possible.

Special thanks to the **open-source community** for their invaluable contributions to machine learning libraries and frameworks. Projects like TensorFlow, Keras, PyTorch, and many others have been instrumental in making advanced machine learning accessible to everyone.

I would also like to acknowledge the support and encouragement of my **readers and learners**. Your curiosity, passion, and feedback have been the driving force behind this book. I hope this guide serves as a valuable resource on your journey to mastering machine learning.

Lastly, I would like to extend my appreciation to my **family and friends** for their unwavering support and understanding throughout this project. Your belief in me has been a constant source of motivation.

Thank you all for being a part of this journey. I look forward to seeing the amazing things you will accomplish with the knowledge and skills gained from this course.